GREGG OLSEN is the New York Times bestselling author of eighteen books, true crime and fiction, including *Fear Collector, A Twisted Faith, Starvation Heights, Abandoned Prayers, If Loving You Is Wrong* and a dozen others. His book *Envy* was Washington State's selection at the National Book Festival in 2012.

REBECCA MORRIS is the New York Times bestselling author of *Bodies of Evidence,* and *If I Can't Have You—Susan Powell, Her Mysterious Disappearance, and the Murder of Her Children* (both with Gregg Olsen). She is also the author of *Ted and Ann—The Mystery of a Missing Child and Her Neighbor Ted Bundy.*

THE GIRL AND THE HORRORS OF HOWARD AVE.

GREGG OLSEN AND REBECCA MORRIS

Copyright 2017 by Gregg Olsen and Rebecca Morris
All Rights Reserved.
Maps by Brad Arnesen
No part of this publication may be reproduced, stored in a retrieval system, or transmitted, in any form or by any means, electronic, mechanical, photocopying, recording, or otherwise, without the written permission of the authors.
Published by Notorious USA

TABLE OF CONTENTS

NOTORIOUS OREGON 7

    INTRODUCTION - TRYING TO AVOID TED, JERRY, RANDY, AND OTHER SERIAL KILLERS BY
    REBECCA MORRIS 9

    ANGELA MCANULTY, THE GIRL AND THE HORRORS OF HOWARD AVENUE 13

    TERRI MOULTON-HORMAN, THE STRANGE DISAPPEARANCE OF KYRON HORMAN 21

    CROOKED RIVER LOVE TWO WOMEN, THEIR ILLICIT LUST, AND THE CHILD MURDERS
        THAT SHOCKED AMERICA 33

    CHRISTIAN LONGO THE NARCISSIST 48

    MY DAY WITH DIANE DOWNS BY GREGG OLSEN 56

    OREGON PHOTO ARCHIVE 61

Notorious Oregon

Introduction
Trying to Avoid Ted, Jerry, Randy, and other Serial Killers
By Rebecca Morris

WHEN I WAS GROWING UP NEAR THE OREGON STATE University campus in Corvallis, Oregon, my bedroom window was above my father's basement workshop. For years I feared someone would stand on the precipice angling out from the workshop and climb into my room.

I didn't have other childhood fears, but I was keenly aware that life could go very, very wrong.

As early as I can remember I heard stories about family tragedies. My maternal grandfather disappeared in the 1920s, leaving his wife and five young children. (He wasn't murdered but it was just as shameful; he ran off with the daughter of the owner of the creamery where he worked. Then he disappeared.) Over and over I heard stories of fluke accidents that took the lives of children who would have grown up to be my older cousins, including a backyard drowning and a truck on a neighborhood street not watching where it was going. A boy I grew up with was found dead floating in the Willamette River. His father was suspected of killing him, but there were no arrests and the case was never solved. When I was still a newlywed, I learned my young husband was going to die of a terrible disease.

In other words, I knew life could turn on a dime and that it's made up of mysteries.

Ted

ONE OF THE BIGGEST MYSTERIES WAS WHO WAS "TED"? IN THE mid-1970s police in the Pacific Northwest were searching for a killer and only had his first name. They knew young women found him handsome; they knew he drove a VW Beetle; and they knew he was suspected of killing college girls in Oregon, Washington, Idaho, and eventually in Colorado and Utah, too.

Roberta Kathleen Parks disappeared from OSU on May 6, 1974. I was a student at Oregon State, but spent that quarter in Portland, interning at a television station. Still, I have a memory of my father, in his seventies, insisting on walking me to an evening class on campus with our family dog, which was big and black but incapable of attacking anyone.

Ted's career as a serial killer and mine as a journalist overlapped. As a reporter in Portland and Seattle, I followed the search for "Ted" and later for other serial killers who traveled Interstate 5, which runs from northern California to British Columbia.

After Ted was executed in 1989 I thought he would finally be just another footnote—although a famous one—in my life as a native of the Northwest. Never in a million years did I think I would write a book about Ted Bundy (*Ted and Ann—The Mystery of a Missing Child and Her Neighbor Ted Bundy*). What was there left to say? Well, there was plenty to say about his first crime. Twenty-two years after he was executed, my book about a missing eight-year old Tacoma girl, Ann Marie Burr, was published. I believe she was Ted's first victim. He was fourteen when she vanished.

Ted was a notable presence in my life during the four years I researched and wrote the book. More than once I dreamed that someone was climbing on to a precipice and trying to enter my bedroom.

Jerry

BEFORE TED, THERE WAS JEROME HENRY BRUDOS, ALSO KNOWN as "The Lust Killer" and "The Shoe Fetish Slayer." He wasn't nearly as good-looking as Ted.

Brudos was born in South Dakota, but his family drifted westward, finally settling in Salem, just twenty miles from Corvallis. His mother reportedly had wanted a girl and dressed Brudos in girl's clothing. By age five he had a thing for women's shoes. He began to stalk women as a teenager, knocking them down or choking them—and stealing their shoes.

After threatening to stab one woman, he spent nine months in the state mental hospital in Salem. He was diagnosed with schizophrenia. And then he was released.

After some training as an electronics technician, he married a seventeen-year-old girl and fathered two children. At one time he worked at a Corvallis radio station, which is creepy since my father spent forty years in what became public radio in Oregon. Brudos came and went frequently from Corvallis since his in-laws lived in my hometown.

I was finishing high school when he killed four young women in 1968 and 1969. He confessed and was sentenced to life in prison. His hobby in prison was collecting women's shoe catalogues. He said it was better than pornography. He died in prison in 2006.

Randy

RANDALL WOODFIELD AND TED BUNDY MIGHT HAVE PASSED each other on the freeway.

Woodfield—called "The I-5 Killer" or "The I-5 Bandit" for the string of murders he committed along the freeway corridor—was convicted of three murders but is suspected of killing dozens.

Born in Salem, Woodfield was a high school football star and attended Portland State University. His coaches looked the other way when he was arrested for indecent exposure.

He might be the only serial killer to be selected in the NFL draft. Despite his arrests in the 1970s for vandalism and public indecency, he was picked by the Green Bay Packers in the fourteenth round of the 1974 draft. The wide receiver was cut during training camp and never played pro football. He did play one season for a semi-pro team.

Between 1979 and 1981, Woodfield robbed gas stations, ice cream parlors and homes, sexually assaulting and murdering some of his victims. While he was charged with four murders, it's estimated he committed as many as forty-four, and dozens of sexual assaults.

He has married three times and divorced twice while in prison in Oregon, where he remains.

Fate led some of us down a different street or into a different store on the days that Ted, Jerry and Randy killed. Some of us were lucky and, tragically, some of us weren't.

Angela McAnulty
The Girl and the Horrors of Howard Avenue

ON THE DAY FIFTEEN-YEAR-OLD JEANETTE MARIE MAPLES DIED, she didn't have a chance to spend time on the few joys she had in life. She didn't compose poetry in her journal. She didn't daydream about growing up to be a chef, librarian, or writer. She didn't fantasize about traveling to France. She didn't play with her German shepherd, Nikita, or breathe in her favorite flower, lilies.

She stopped breathing sometime on December 9, 2009 after being beaten, chained to a bed, and put in a bathtub of cold water.

Which was not new. Jeanette Maples had been intentionally maimed, starved and tortured for years by her mother.

WE KNOW MORE ABOUT THE TORTURE JEANETTE ENDURED than we know about her.

The few people who saw her the last years of her life, her step-grandmother and younger half-sister, say she was a quiet, shy, teen with brown hair. Although Jeanette often seemed bruised and hungry, in photographs she smiled through unrelenting psychological and physical pain. She had warm eyes and tilted her head when she smiled, showing dimples.

Jeanette won two awards for perfect attendance at Cascade Middle School in Eugene, Oregon. For the last two years of her life, her mother kept her at home, supposedly home-schooling her. What she really received were lessons in horror.

On Jeannette's last day of life, Jeannette passed out from being beaten and starved. When the bathtub of water didn't revive her, her mother, Angela McAnulty, called her mother-in-law, who had been concerned about ongoing abuse in the house. Angela told her that Jeanette had stopped breathing.

Lynn McAnulty screamed at her daughter-in-law, trying to get her attention.

"Angela! Call 9-1-1! For God's sake, call 9-1-1!"

When paramedics arrived at the ranch house on Howard Avenue just after 8 p.m. they found a child so frail and emaciated they could see her bones. She was so small they couldn't believe she was a teenager.

Someone had moved her from the bathtub to the living room floor. She had no shirt on, her hair was wet, and she had bruises on her face and cuts above her eye.

"Help my baby!" Angela pleaded with the first responders. She explained that Jeanette had fallen down and about an hour later began to feel sick.

The girl had no pulse. Paramedics tried CPR and put a tube into her lungs in an effort to help her breathe. Her mother stood nearby, alternating between silence and hysteria. She even laughed a couple of times.

"I just remember it was an odd response," Fire Captain Sven Wahlroos said. "Very odd." It was so odd that it made the hair on the back of his neck stand up. "I have never had that feeling in eighteen years," he said. "All I wanted to do was run."

He called the police. When they arrived they found blood on the walls of a bedroom, with a bucket of "reddish soapy water" nearby. Angela eventually acknowledged striking Jeanette with a belt and a sewing yardstick. She said she tried to fix the girl's wounds with iodine and bandages, even though they were so severe you could see bone.

Emergency room physicians at Sacred Heart Medical Center-Riverbend, in the Eugene suburb of Springfield, were told by Jeanette's mother that the girl had no previous medical problems. But they found cuts and wounds on Jeanette's lips that were old and appeared never to have been treated. Her front teeth were broken. There were severe wounds on her legs and back. She had an exposed femur.

It was clear she had been tortured for years. She was pronounced dead at 8:42 p.m.

It's the most horrific of crimes. How could a mother torture her child to death? The answer may be in Angela McAnulty's own childhood, which was one long nightmare.

Angela grew up in California and was just five when her mother was murdered. After the tragedy, Angela lived with her father and two brothers. The murder of her mother was never solved, but her father was always the prime suspect. Not surprisingly, his children were afraid of him.

He starved and beat his children to punish them. "We weren't allowed to get food out of the kitchen at all, we knew that," Angela's brother, Mike Feusi, later testified. "We could get water but that was it." The boys were physically abused by their father and suspected that Angela was sexually abused by him.

After high school, Angela ran off with a carnival worker. She eventually had five children by three men. Her sons, Anthony Jr. and Brandon, as well as Jeanette, were fathered by Anthony Maples. Angela and Anthony never married, and both were both arrested on drug charges and spent time in prison. During that time, the three children were in foster care.

After Angela got out of prison, she regained custody of Jeanette, who by then had spent six of the first seven years of childhood in foster care. Angela gave birth to another daughter fathered by an unknown man and named the baby Patience. Then she met Richard McAnulty. They had a boy, Richard Jr., and the family moved to Oregon in 2006. Angela's two oldest sons, Anthony Jr. and Brandon, elected to stay in foster care in California.

In Oregon, Angela worked as a cashier at a discount store and Richard as a truck driver. Their house was filthy, with junk and toys crowding the rooms. Angela forced Jeanette to sleep on a piece of cardboard on the floor to prevent her bloody wounds from ruining a mattress.

IN ANCIENT CIVILIZATIONS, INFANTICIDE WAS LEGAL. Mothers killed their children because they were illegitimate, crippled or mentally abnormal.

Today it is the most horrific of crimes. Yet there are only two crimes that women in the U.S. commit as frequently as men: shoplifting and the murder of their own children.

The cases and the trials are covered in detail by cable television. Susan Smith and Diane Downs killed their children because they believed they were impediments to relationships with boyfriends. Andrea Yates suffered from severe postpartum depression. Casey Anthony most likely covered up an accident that occurred because she had neglected her daughter. Amy Grossberg and Brian Peterson left their newborn in a Dumpster, and claimed—falsely—that the baby was stillborn.

The most common form of child murder is neonaticide, the killing of a newborn within twenty-four hours of birth. The next is infanticide, the killing of an infant under the age of one. Filicide is the killing of an older child by a parent.

And then there is a crime with no name except just plain murder: the torture of a child until they die, committed by parents who for some inexplicable reason single out one of their children to abuse and neglect. Like other mothers who have committed this most notorious of crimes, Angela McAnulty had a childhood that was a blueprint for her own parenting. She had been deprived of nutrition as a child; she had probably been sexually abused; she had used drugs; she lived at or near the poverty level; she hadn't had much education; and she lacked emotional support.

There's an axiom about that kind of childhood.

Those who were abused, abuse.

Jeannette Marie Maples was buried on December 17, 2009. Her mother and stepfather were absent. They were busy being arraigned in Lane County Circuit Court on murder charges.

Angela Darlene McAnulty, forty-one, was charged with aggravated murder for essentially torturing, beating and starving Jeanette to death. The wording the State of Oregon used was "intentional maiming and torture."

Jeanette's stepfather, forty-year-old Richard McAnulty, was also charged with murder. Prosecutors said he failed to prevent or report his wife's torture and abuse, and helped to enforce her restrictions on Jeanette's food and water.

On the first day of her trial on February 1, 2011, Angela McAnulty pleaded guilty to the charges. After a hearing, a jury would decide if she would be given the death penalty.

Angela did not take the witness stand, but made a personal statement to the jury considering whether to sentence her to death. She acknowledged fatally abusing her daughter, but added: "I did not want my little girl to die." Because she didn't testify, she couldn't be cross-examined by prosecutors.

Her mother-in-law, Lynn McAnulty, testified that she had repeatedly called a state child-abuse hotline—anonymously—hoping to get someone to check on her step-granddaughter. She became concerned after seeing the girl with a split and swollen lip.

"And it looked like somebody had taken a fist and yanked her hair," she told the jury.

When she asked her son and daughter-in-law about the injuries, she was told Jeanette had "fallen down." In hindsight, she admitted she should have called police.

The only eyewitness to Jeanette's life of agony was her younger half-sister, thirteen-year-old Patience. The girl told the jury that their mother's harsh treatment of her older sister began as soon as Angela regained custody of Jeanette. The last few days of her life, Patience said, Jeanette was "acting kind of strange." She was speaking incoherently and when she was punished by being ordered to stand with her face to the wall and her hands extended over her head, she fell. She was confined to a bedroom in the back of the house, away from the family. Patience was forbidden to talk to her sister but tried to sneak water to her. If she was caught, their mother retaliated by yelling at Patience and beating Jeanette.

The jury heard the gruesome details: Angela had punished Jeanette by depriving her of food and water, hit her with shoes, and hit her on the mouth with the back of her hand, sometimes drawing blood. She smeared dog feces on Jeanette's face. Authorities called it one of the worst cases of child abuse they'd ever seen.

As for Jeanette's stepfather, his lawyer cited Richard McAnulty's low IQ and his curious adulthood as explanations for how he looked the other way while Jeanette was tortured. According to his attorney, he had lived at home with his mother, who made all his decisions, until he was thirty-two and married Angela. Then his wife took over, running his life and "manipulating" him. According to testimony, on the evening Jeanette died Angela wanted to bury the body without calling authorities, but McAnulty stopped her. Prosecutors did not seek the death penalty in his case.

The state of Oregon failed Jeanette Maples. A child welfare caseworker testified that she never got a full picture of the family's history in California. She knew that Angela had met the state's requirements for getting her daughter back, including negative drug tests. Her two sons, Jeanette's older brothers, had refused to go back to their mom and elected to stay in foster care. They were lucky that they were old enough to make that decision. Jeanette wasn't.

There were at least four reports to Oregon's child welfare division during the last three years of Jeanette's life, one just a week before she died. But caseworkers failed to intervene. No one was fired as a result of the case, but employees were disciplined and one worker was reassigned.

In 2011, a Portland lawyer filed a wrongful death suit against the Oregon Department of Human Services, alleging that state officials could have prevented the girl's death. Oregon agreed to pay $1.5 million to Jeanette's father, Anthony Maples, who was reportedly "crushed" when he got the phone call telling him of his daughter's death.

"It's not like I need the money," he said. "It's almost like I don't want the money because of where it came from. I know that's hard to fathom."

It *is* hard to fathom, because Maples hadn't seen his daughter in ten years. His last memory of her was when they went to see a movie, he thinks it was *Atlantis: The Lost Empire*, an animated film about a young adventurer. "She was so happy being with her father. I remember her smile and her giggle," he said.

Jeanette's step-grandmother, Lynn McAnulty, said Maples didn't deserve to benefit from his daughter's death.

JURIES DON'T LIKE TO CONDEMN MOTHERS TO DEATH. But on February 24, 2011, Angela McAnulty became just the second woman in state history to face execution.

The first was Jeannace Freeman. Called "the most despised criminal in all of Oregon," Freeman was just nineteen years old in 1961 when she helped thirty-three-year-old Gertrude Jackson strangle, bludgeon and throw her two children into the Crooked River Gorge in Central Oregon. Freeman's death sentence was commuted after Oregon voters abolished capital punishment. She served more than twenty years in prison. Jackson served just seven years.

Angela McAnulty, forty-four, is at the Coffee Creek Correctional Facility in Wilsonville, the only women's prison in Oregon. She has years of appeals ahead of her. And, as other death row inmates have learned over the years, Oregon often changes its mind about executing people. Since the 1960s, voters have both restored and repealed capital punishment numerous times. There's a death penalty, but Oregon's governor has issued a moratorium on executions on his watch.

Richard McAnulty was sentenced to life in prison and will serve a minimum of twenty-five years. Now forty-three, he resides at the Snake River Correctional Institution in Ontario, Oregon.

As for their other children, the couple gave up custody of their eight-year-old son, clearing the way for him to be adopted. Patience, Angela's thirteen-year-old daughter, who bravely testified at her stepfather's trial, is in foster care. After her mother and stepfather were sentenced, she thanked her friends, foster family and others for "cheering me on from near and far."

She has an unusually mature and optimistic outlook on her life. "I think my childhood is not ruined, but depressing," she said. "I am slowly healing."

Jeanette's birth father and two older brothers weren't at her funeral. Neither were her two younger half-siblings, who had been taken into state custody after their parents' arrests. Jeanette's step-grandparents, Richard McAnulty's parents, attended, along with a cousin. Most of the people in attendance, including a deputy district attorney and a hospital chaplain, only knew Jeanette after she died.

A classmate from Cascade Middle School who had been Jeannette's lab partner in Biology class, said she wished she had known the girl better. After speaking, she sat in a pew alone and cried.

Another girl and her mother sang a Martina McBride song about an abused child, titled "Concrete Angel." It's about a lonely girl who hides her bruises; neighbors hear her but ignore her cries until it's too late.

Terri Moulton-Horman
The Strange Disappearance of Kyron Horman

THE BOY WITH THE TOOTHY SMILE, CREWCUT AND GLASSES posed in front of his science project, three cardboard walls with a small diorama at its base. It was everything a boy would ever want to know about the red-eyed tree frog.

It was Friday, June 4, 2010, and seven-year-old Kyron Horman was proud of his contribution to the science fair at Portland's Skyline Elementary School. In addition to illustrating the frog's life cycle, the project explained that the rain-forest amphibian developed its huge scarlet peepers to shock predators. If a bird or snake got too close—and hesitated a moment before striking—the tree frog flashed its bulging eyes, webbed orange feet and neon-green body, giving it a precious second to jump to safety.

But safety depended on the bird or snake hesitating. Often the tree frog was attacked anyway.

Kyron, a shy second-grader who loved science, bowling, and fishing, was showing his display to a different breed of predator, a member of the human species, his stepmother, Terri Horman. The school had opened early so parents and children could see the exhibits.

Kyron grinned for Terri's camera. Then, at 8:45 a.m., Terri said goodbye and watched as Kyron walked down the hallway to his first class, math.

Or so she said.

TV VIEWERS KNOW THAT THE FIRST FORTY-EIGHT HOURS of an investigation into a missing person is the most important time. For children, it's the first *two* hours. Kyron wasn't reported missing for six long hours.

Terri had borrowed her husband's white Ford F250 pickup for

the day. After she left Kyron at school, she went to the Fred Meyer in Hillsboro around nine a.m. and another Fred Meyer on Walker Road in Beaverton at 10 a.m. At one of the stores she ran into a former manager of her gym, who said Terri showed her pictures of Kyron at the science fair. The woman said it was odd because she'd never really talked to Terri before, and now she was going on and on as if to make a point. Then Terri drove around for an hour and a half in an attempt to soothe her toddler, Kiara, who had an earache, and stopped at her gym for forty-five minutes to work out.

By 1:21 p.m. she was home posting photos of Kyron on Facebook. A former teacher and body builder, her Facebook page also had pictures of her when she was blonde, tan, and muscular, posing in a blue bikini for a bodybuilding competition.

At 3:30 p.m., Terri, Kyron's father, Kaine, and little Kiara went to meet the school bus. But Kyron wasn't on the bus. His parents called the school, and the school notified the police. Terri called the boy's biological mother, Desiree Young, in Medford, Oregon.

Kyron's school admitted it hadn't known the boy was missing. There appeared to be a mix-up because Terri had said something vague about a doctor's appointment. Later, she told police that the appointment was actually scheduled for June 11, a week after the boy went missing.

At 4:33 p.m., officers from the Portland Police Bureau and the Multnomah County Sheriff's Office arrived simultaneously at Skyline School and the Horman home. About an hour later, an alert was sent to parents in the school district notifying them that there was a student missing.

Kaine told police he last saw his son at about 7:45 a.m. Kyron had just fed their cat Bootsie and on his way out the door to work, Kaine told him how proud of him he was for his work on the red-eyed tree frog project. They hugged, the father told his son he loved him, and the son said he loved his dad, too.

That evening, officers searched the school and the Horman home, the FBI was informed, and investigators began talking to the media and handing out photos of Kyron. They said he was wearing a "CSI" t-shirt, black cargo pants, Hanes athletic socks, and well-worn Skechers sneakers.

Long into the night, police with trained dogs combed the woods and farmland near the school. Within a few days, thirteen hundred searchers were joined by more than 200 additional investigators from other agencies in Oregon, California, and Washington. It would be the largest search operation in Oregon history.

But critical hours were lost. A former FBI profiler told the media that the investigation got underway "eight to twelve hours after it should have."

THE FOCUS OF THE INVESTIGATION QUICKLY BECAME Kyron's stepmother—and how she had spent her time the morning he vanished.

There were gaps in what Terri Horman told investigators she did that day, including the key portion of time that she said she took Kiara for a ride. Terri told investigators that she drove Kiara around a series of rural roads, trying to calm her down because Kiara didn't feel well.

The Multnomah County Sheriff's Office—the lead agency in the case—confirmed that Terri had been to the two grocery stores and the gym but her cell phone records didn't match up with other parts of her story. They began to focus on whether anyone else was with her. At least two witnesses believed they saw an adult waiting in the truck while Terri was inside the school with Kyron. Her friends were questioned and some of them were given polygraphs.

The investigation led police to DeDe Spicher, one of three friends of Terri's who used fake names to buy prepaid cell phones in the days after Kyron disappeared. She had known the Hormans for about seven years and used to work out with Terri. On blogs, Spicher described herself as a "fitness junkie, med school wannabe, and pet-sitting veteran" who was "passionate about organic gardening."

On the day Kyron disappeared, DeDe Spicher was working at a

nursery near the Hormans house. Police determined that she was missing for three hours at the same time Terri was supposedly driving rural roads. Two people, including her employer, tried to reach her on her cell phone during those hours but she didn't answer. Spicher's car, however, had been left at the job site. Someone had picked her up.

On June 5, the day after Kyron disappeared, Spicher responded to a tweet about the boy's disappearance: She wrote, *This is my friend's child. I know him. It's so scary!*

A newspaper article called Kyron's parents and step-parents a "close, supportive group."

It was really a blended family that never quite got the mix right.

Kyron was born to Kaine Horman and Desiree Horman on September 9, 2002 at St. Vincent's Hospital in Portland. It was Desiree's second marriage and she also had a seven-year-old son. Kyron's birth was not without drama. Kaine and Desiree were in the midst of a divorce, Desiree was pregnant, Kaine was having an affair with Terri, and Desiree had filed for a restraining order against him. In court documents, she said she feared that her soon-to-be ex-husband would "remove our children from their residence." A judge granted Desiree Young's request, forbidding either her or Kaine Horman from taking the children without the other's consent.

For his first two years, Kyron lived with Desiree in Portland. He went to live with Kaine and his new wife, Terri—who Desiree blamed for the breakup of her marriage—when Desiree was hospitalized with kidney failure. Desiree later moved to southern Oregon and married Tony Young, a detective in Medford, and shared custody with Kaine. Kyron visited Desiree often. On recent visits, Kyron cried and resisted going back to Kaine and Terri's, Desiree said.

Kaine and Terri Moulton married in 2007; it was her third marriage. Terri had a sixteen-year-old son by her first husband who had been adopted by her second husband. She and Kaine had daughter Kiara in December, 2008.

Kaine was doing reasonably well. An engineer for Intel, he earned about $90,000 the year Kyron was born and the family lived in a house off a secluded road in the woods northwest of Portland. The very modest split-level was assessed at $292,000. On Mother's Day, 2007, Kaine gave his new bride a candy-apple red Ford Mustang GT. *Something shiny for the driveway*, Terri wrote under the picture on her Facebook page. *Yes, Kaine is all that and a bag of chips!* Her vanity license plate read RDSQRL, short for Red Squirrel, a nickname given her because of her long, thick mane of red hair.

In the early days after Kyron vanished, the two couples stood together and made pleas through the media for the boy's safe return. Because the Multnomah County Sheriff's Office said the more familiar people became with the second-grader, the better the chances were of finding him, they talked about how, in addition to science and tree frogs, Kyron liked to get dirty and loved miniature golf and camping.

The four, all in their late thirties and early forties, made an attractive picture. Kaine's light hair, crew cut and widow's peak were just like Kyron's. With her red hair loose down her back, Terri looked to be grieving and often had her head on her husband's chest as they talked to reporters. She had grown plump since her bodybuilding days. Desiree, with long, blonde hair—sometimes curled, sometimes blown straight—was striking, prettier than her former nemesis. With his short dark hair and solid build, her husband Tony Young, the Medford cop, seemed to shore up the others.

They all wore t-shirts with Kyron's photo and the word Missing in large orange letters. They seem united. There was an even an awkward moment when Terri tried to comfort Desiree in front of the TV cameras. But when the stepmom put an arm around the mom and tried to rest her head on her shoulder, Desiree responded by clenching her hands together in front of her.

Whether it was genuine or not, that try at intimacy was shattered as soon as investigators began focusing on Terri Horman.

Police prepared flyers that had photographs of the white truck, Terri, and DeDe Spicher, hoping someone had seen the truck and the women.

Kaine, Desiree and Tony Young became suspicious of Terri. She balked at being grilled by the police when the others were freely doing all they could to help. The four adults all took polygraphs and Terri did not "pass" hers. She vented about the results to family, friends and law enforcement at the house. A few days later she agreed to a second one, but got up and walked out before it was finished. Police said Terri knew something she wasn't divulging. Kaine and Desiree believed Terri had failed two or three polygraphs. Police, and the boy's parents learned, that Terri had lied about watching Kyron walk to his classroom and waving to him from a staircase. Logistically, it couldn't have happened. The classroom wasn't visible from the staircase.

Kaine later told reporters, "We'd be working with investigators, we would be doing everything that we could and just in the natural course of our actions she was separating herself... it was just apparent that the three of us were driving to find him and she was not."

Desiree Young said she had felt uneasy ever since Terri had phoned to say that Kyron was missing. She said Terri seemed surprised that Desiree was dropping everything to drive north to Portland.

"Honestly, my motherly instinct kicked in, and I said that she better not have done anything to my son," Young said. "I just didn't feel right about the conversation. It didn't strike me right."

SAUVIE ISLAND IS 26,000 ACRES OF NARROW ROADS, FARMLAND and wildlife refuge. Larger than Manhattan, the island is just ten miles northwest of Portland at the confluence of two great rivers, the Columbia and Willamette. Only thirteen hundred people live on the island, but a million people a year visit the beaches and cycle, hike and pick blueberries.

Searchers covered Sauvie Island more than once after learning that pings from Terri's cell phone indicated she may have been on the island the day Kyron disappeared—a location reportedly at odds with her own account of her movements that day.

A sheriff's posse on horseback went house to house looking for Kyron, and rode through orchards, farm fields and pumpkin patches while an Oregon National Guard UH-60 Black Hawk helicopter flew overhead.

There was no sign of Kyron.

Over the weeks they used dogs and horses to search thousands of acres of private timberland on mountain roads, although they had to wait for snow to melt. They also searched Spicher's suburban condo, the garden property on Northwest Old Germantown Road where Spicher was working that day, and a relative's address as they sought to determine Spicher's movements.

ONCE THE BOMBSHELLS BEGAN, THEY NEVER SEEMED TO STOP. In late June, police learned that Terri had reportedly tried to hire someone—six months before Kyron disappeared—to kill Kaine. She had asked a landscaper who had been working on their property if he would kill her husband for "a large sum of money." Terri told him she was in a bad marriage and that Kaine had "hurt" her. On June 26, police set up a sting. The landscaper, wearing a wire, met with Terri and took along an undercover officer posing as his buddy.

Police were ready to arrest Terri if she implicated herself, but she cut the conversation short.

Later that day, Kaine was told that she had tried to have him killed. He immediately took their nineteen-month-old daughter and moved out. Two days later, Kaine said Terri attempted to kidnap Kiara. He got a restraining order and filed for divorce. In response, Terri said she had nothing to do with Kyron's disappearance, had received death threats and complained that the case had morphed into a "witch hunt." She hired Stephen Houze, a well-known Oregon lawyer often referred to as the top criminal defense attorney in the state. Somehow she raised $350,000 to retain him.

After Kaine moved out of his house, Terri Horman's good friend DeDe Spicher moved in.

Four days after Kaine left the house, Terri Horman began "sexting" a man Kaine had gone to high school with. Michael Cook had shown up at the Horman house after they were in the news because of Kyron's disappearance. Kaine said it was the first time he'd seen him in years. Cook began visiting Terri at the house after Kaine left. It wasn't the shocking inappropriateness of his relationship with Terri that led police to question Michael Cook. It was that Terri had shared confidential information from a sealed restraining order with Cook, allowing him to map the address where Kaine was living with Kiara. Then he shared the address with at least two other people.

Law enforcement found hundreds of text messages between Terri Horman and Cook, as well as photographs of Terri "in various stages of undress and graphic sexual activity" on Cook's cell phone, and they shared the information with Kaine.

By July, Terri had moved back to her parents' home in Roseburg, Oregon and Kaine and Kiara had moved back into their house.

TIME PASSED WITH NO SIGN OF KYRON. A year after he was last seen, the Multnomah County Sheriff's Office disbanded its special task force created to look for the boy. Detectives that had been loaned to the task force went back to their respective agencies. Sheriff Dan Staton promised it would not become a cold case and said his office would continue to investigate, with the help of the FBI and state and county prosecutors. The sheriff said they had looked at sixty persons of interest, including known sex offenders and visitors to the school the day of the science fair.

Terri Moulton Horman remained the focus of the investigation.

But with no indictment and no arrest, Desiree Young turned to civil court, filing a $10 million lawsuit against Terri. The suit contended Kyron's stepmother kidnapped the boy and asked that she be compelled to bring him back or divulge where his body was taken.

Young's attorney said the lawsuit would enable him to subpoena witnesses, acquire documents and evidence and "peel away the mystery" of what happened to Kyron. DeDe Spicher, for example, could be compelled to testify.

It is a legal move sometimes pursued to circumvent a stalled police investigation or after a less than satisfactory verdict (for example, when the parents of Ronald Goldman sued O. J. Simpson after he was acquitted of murder).

The lawsuit got underway but the woman expected to implicate Terri Horman, DeDe Spicher, cited her Fifth Amendment right against self-incrimination in a deposition, refusing to answer more than 100 questions—including whether she even knew Terri, Kaine, and Desiree or had ever met Kyron. She did tell Desiree Young's lawyers that she, too, had left Portland and had moved to her parents' house in Klamath Falls, Oregon in September 2010 after losing her job. In Klamath Falls she went to work at a medical clinic, helping coordinate patients' referrals to specialists.

Before the case could go much further, a judge halted the case, saying it could impact the ongoing criminal investigation. He did, however, go further than the sheriff's office had gone. He called Terri Horman a "prime suspect" in Kyron's disappearance.

More than three years after his son vanished, Kaine Horman's divorce from Terri Moulton Horman wasn't wrapped up, either. Kaine's attorneys asked the court to delay the divorce, believing that, like the postponement of the civil suit, it would be in the best interest of the criminal investigation. Court documents filed by the Multnomah County Sheriff and district attorney in January 2013, said that delaying the divorce case would allow investigators to move forward "without interference."

Terri Horman continued to deny her involvement in her stepson's disappearance. A close friend of Terri's told a Portland TV station that she is a wonderful mother who had known Kyron since he was three days old. She said the scrutiny has taken an emotional toll on her.

If Terri was responsible for her stepson's disappearance, the question is: why? Was she jealous of Kyron? Was she tired of helping raise another woman's child? Kaine Horman said there was never any indication that his wife had negative feelings toward Kyron. But that was before he learned that Terri had sent e-mails to a family member expressing her hatred for the boy. He knew her behavior had started to change in 2005, he thought she drank too much, and she had been on medication for postpartum depression after Kiara was born. Kaine said he and Terri had discussed separating before Kyron disappeared, but had worked through the problems in a "positive manner."

Despite making his own mistakes, Kaine is portrayed in the media sympathetically as a tortured father single-mindedly focused on finding his son. He's never addressed the sordid details that have come out about his own life—how he was having an affair with Terri while still married to a pregnant Desiree, how Desiree got a restraining order against Kaine, and how in 2008, his thirty-two-year-old brother was arrested and convicted of molesting a former stepdaughter. The brother told police there was a history of abuse in the Horman family and said his grandfather had abused him.

DESIREE YOUNG AND KAINE HORMAN continue to believe that one day Kyron will come home.

She's disappointed that her civil suit against Terri Horman is on hold, but keeps the pressure on Terri by sending messages via the media. On ABC's *Good Morning America* Desiree told Terri to "do the right thing" and bring Kyron home, warning her that "you will go to jail, and whoever has been helping you, if they don't talk, they will go to jail."

Desiree has kept her son's room in her Medford, Oregon home just as it was the last weekend he visited. She has left his bed unmade. The cars he was playing with cover the floor.

But Kaine has changed Kyron's room in the Portland house, removing toys the seven-year old enjoyed and replacing them with video games an older boy would like. He also buys his son new clothes, expecting him to be taller and bigger when he comes home.

Kaine was encouraged by the May 2013 discovery of three girls who had been confined to a house in Ohio for ten years. He expects Kyron to one day be among the children who've been found after lengthy periods of time. He said he has no reason to believe his son is not still alive.

He thinks that if foul play was involved, Kyron would have been found by now. Until he knows otherwise, Kaine Horman said, "He's going to be brought home. It's just a matter of when."

KYRON'S PARENTS HADN'T SPOKEN FOR NEARLY THREE YEARS when they appeared on *Dr. Phil* on September 17, 2013.

Desiree Young said she didn't blame her ex-husband for their son's disappearance, but claimed he knew of Terri Horman's dislike of Kyron. Desiree said that when Kaine was traveling on business, Terri would call her asking her to drive the four hours and get Kyron. But Kaine opposed any change in their custody arrangement.

The night before Kyron disappeared, Terri Horman reportedly e-mailed friends that she and Kaine had argued until 3 a.m. and that she planned to leave him. Kaine said on *Dr. Phil* that the incident never happened. But Desiree Young feels that if Terri Horman is responsible for Kyron's disappearance, her motive was to get even with Kaine.

Phil McGraw encouraged the parents to put their differences aside. "Be mad at each other later. You need to work together to find this child," he said.

Desiree feels strongly that Kaine knew Terri posed a threat to Kyron. But she feels responsibility, too.

"I won't forgive myself for not pushing for custody," Desiree said tearfully. "We failed Kyron."

The Kyron Horman Tip Line: 503-261-2847

For more information: www.bringkyronhome.org

Crooked River Love
Two Women, Their Illicit Lust, and the Child Murders That Shocked America

JUST BEFORE SUNRISE ON THURSDAY, MAY 11, 1961, A CREAM-colored, two-door 1952 Mercury with red wheels pulled off Highway 97 at a wayside at Crooked River Canyon, a volcanic gorge that had split central Oregon in two for 1.6 million years. Nineteen-year-old Jeannace June Freeman was behind the wheel. With her hair slicked back and her breasts bound, Freeman could pass as a young man, and usually did. In the passenger seat was thirty-three-year-old Gertrude May Nunez Jackson. She was small, just about five feet tall, weighed 100 pounds and had dark short curly hair. More than Jeannace, Gertrude resembled the women of rural Oregon in their dresses, aprons and pedal pushers.

Soon, the farm wives would crowd their county's proud, new courthouse to hear the salacious details of a story about sex, race and murder.

Asleep in the backseat were Gertrude's two children, six-year-old Lawrence and four-year-old Martha. The children had a dark complexion and their mother sometimes told people they were Portuguese. Before their broken and bloody bodies were positively identified, police speculated they were French or Mexican. But Larry and Marty, as they were called, were the offspring of their white mother and her common-law husband, a drug-addicted "Negro" (as African-Americans were called then).

In 1961, any kind of marital or sexual union between a white and a Negro was still illegal in some states and considered abhorrent in most.

Jeannace and Gertrude had met a few weeks earlier in Eugene, Oregon, when Gertrude was in need of a babysitter and was introduced to Jeannace by a neighbor. For the first week or two, Gertrude believed that Jeannace *was* a young man. Gertrude had an undiagnosed mental illness and was vulnerable. Half-heartedly on her part, the two became lovers. Jeannace accompanied Gertrude and the children when they returned to where they had been living, Oakland, California. But Jeannace's restlessness returned, and after a couple of weeks the two women and the children headed back north to Oregon.

By the time the car reached the Crooked River Canyon, their ardor had cooled. Jeannace would tell at least six versions of what happened that night, but one detail that popped up in all of them was that the children were getting in the way of what remained of their relationship. Jeannace started the conversation, but Gertrude listened. Jeannace's suggestions included leaving Larry and Marty in caves near the California-Oregon border or lighting them on fire with kerosene to make identifying them harder.

As they drove north, Jeannace realized she knew the perfect spot. She had grown up a house near the Crooked River Canyon. Two miles upstream of the bridge was where she learned to fish.

Jeannace drove into the small park at the south end of the bridge that crossed the canyon. She backed the Mercury up to a retaining wall, kissed Gertrude, and talked of how later, after the murders, they would rest up at her stepfather's house and go fishing in the afternoon.

They left the children sleeping in the back seat and walked along the waist-high wall. It was Gertrude's first visit and as the sun started to rise she could see the spectacular drop. It was 360 feet of jagged volcanic rock from top to bottom, twenty-seven stories deep. It was said that if you threw a match over the side, it would ignite from the friction caused by speed and height.

The women looked for a spot where the wall was flush, with no rocky precipices that could snag a small body. Then one or both of them strangled Larry, undressed him, bludgeoned his head with a tire iron, ripped open his rectum with it, and threw him over the rim. One or both of them then undressed Marty, used the tire iron on her vagina, and threw her over the wall. Just as she was released, the girl grabbed for her mother. Marty landed on her feet, crumpled, and lived for about a minute.

When her body was found, she was still clutching some of her mother's hair in her tiny fist.

They weren't the first deaths at the Crooked River Canyon, and they wouldn't be the last. But Oregon and the rest of the country held a special hatred for the two women. There was talk of lynching and throwing *them* off the bridge. The closest a jury could come to old-fashioned western justice was to make certain that for the first time ever, a woman was executed in Oregon.

Jeannace Freeman and Gertrude Jackson were condemned as much for being lovers as for the murder of two children.

Jeannace Freeman boasted that she could turn any woman into a lesbian in fifteen minutes.

It took her a week or two to seduce Gertrude. It was another story with many versions. Either Gertrude asked for a kiss, or Jeannace took the initiative. Two days later they made love on Gertrude's living room floor. At some point Letha L___, a friend of Jeannace's, broke the news to Gertrude that Jeannace was a woman.

Jeannace (pronounced Jen-ACE) could look like a young man. At nineteen, she was five-foot-three weighed less than 120 pounds, and had short, curly, dark brown hair and blue eyes. When she flattened her breasts and wore cowboy boots, a man's hat, a western-style jacket, tight-fitting jeans and walked with a swagger, many assumed she was a cocky young male. Presumably, Gertrude saw Jeannace's tattoos: Spinner over her left breast; Julia over her right breast; Lucky and Tiger on her arms. And there were more. After she was arrested in California, police said she had disguised herself as a man to "escape detection." They were wrong.

She just liked looking and acting like a man. Maybe because life as a girl had disappointed her.

Her father was killed in a car accident when she was young and her stepfather—Clyde Witcraft, known as "Red"—began raping her when she was four. He also spent time in prison for raping neighbor girls. Her family called her "Jen" or "Jenny," but strangers thinking her "mannish" thought her name was "Gene." She was one of ten children born to her mother, who left her and her two half-brothers behind when she left Red.

Jeannace's first love affair was at age twelve, when she traded sex for the affection of an older girl. She was expelled from school and spent some time in a foster home. When she was fourteen, she stole a pistol and a car, held up a Portland store, and drove home to central Oregon. She was arrested for armed robbery and sent to Hillcrest, the reform school for girls in Oregon. Her records state that she had "homosexual relations with many other inmates" and was labeled a "sexual deviate." That's probably where she met Letha, who would become a lover and sometime roommate.

GERTRUDE NUNEZ JACKSON had a difficult life before she met Jeannace, but things quickly went from bad to worse after they met. If women had let Jeannace down, it was men who had disappointed Gertrude. She was born in The Dalles, grew up in Portland and Eugene, and ran away to Seattle with a soldier when she was sixteen after a fight in a restaurant with her sister; Gertrude claimed they were both trying to seduce the same man.

She married a Mexican—most likely not the soldier—named Gregorio Nunez. They moved to California where she worked in canneries and laundries and he was a day laborer. The couple would go drinking with Dempsey Otis Jackson, a black man, and a second woman. A couple of years later, Gertrude left Gregorio—and a four-year-old son—to live with Jackson. She gave birth to Larry and Marty. She never divorced Nunez but considered Jackson her husband.

Gertrude and the children were never settled for long, sometimes living in Oakland, sometimes in Eugene. D.O. Jackson was not with them. She thought she could give them a better life with no man around. But when she met Jeannace, the children had been sick and so was Gertrude—she had an infected tumor pressing on her spine. Her plans to make a go of it alone with Larry and Marty got put aside after Gertrude and the children, along with Jeannace and Letha, moved back to Oakland. Gertrude always worked, even sick, so Jeannace watched the two children. When she could afford to, Gertrude hired a babysitter anyway because Jeannace wasn't the most reliable babysitter or the best influence on the kids.

In early May, Jeannace wrote her family that she was coming for a visit and several days later they all piled into Gertrude's Mercury and headed to Oregon. When they stopped in Klamath Falls to see Jeannace's mother, the children were with them. They dropped Letha at her parents in Cottage Grove, south of Eugene, and then continued north.

SEVENTEEN-YEAR-OLD RONN WITCRAFT AWOKE TO A POUNDING on the door of the house. He and his fifteen-year-old brother, Tom, were Jeannace's half-brothers and lived with their dad, Red Witcraft. It was a messy family life. Ronn and Tom were among the ten children born to Jeannace's mother. Their father had seven children from four wives. Ronn's own sexual history began in first grade when he had sex with an adult woman. He said that there wasn't anything he didn't know about sex by age six or seven.

Despite knowing that his dad had raped Jen—his favorite sister—and other girls, Ronn held a high opinion of his father, especially family dinners when Red focused on his sons. "We'd always sit down and talk about things. He was a good judge of human character," Ronn said.

May 11 was "a day you can't forget," Ronn said years later. It was 5:45 a.m. and it was his sister knocking on the door of the house in Culver, a wide spot in the road a few miles northwest of the bridge. They wanted to clean their car, get a few hours of sleep, and go fishing.

Jeannace introduced Gertrude and said she was "blue" because she had left her children in foster care in Portland. Tom helped them clean the car. There was the general stuff that accumulates on a car trip, including Dairy Queen paper cups and other refuse. But they had to use warm soapy water to wash out the trunk and back seat. One of the women took a bag of something inside the house and insisted on burning it in the wood stove.

After a breakfast of hotcakes, Jen gave the boys a ride in the car and Tom and Ronn left for school. Gertrude cashed a $4 income tax refund check and bought cigarettes and beer. Red made a pass at her but she turned him down. The three of them went fishing and that night there was fried fish for dinner.

Just before they set out the next morning, Jen asked a question.

"She asked how to head down Highway 97 without going over the bridge," Ronn said. Red explained a route that that would take them east on Highway 26 to Prineville where they could turn south and get back on Highway 97. It bypassed the Crooked River Bridge. The women left.

At 3 p.m. Friday, more than thirty hours after the children landed at the bottom of the gorge, a car with three forest service employees stopped on the way back from a conference at Timberline Lodge on Mount Hood. One of men, Walter H. Meyer Jr., looked over the ledge and spotted what at first seemed to be two dolls at the bottom of the canyon. The men talked it over and decided they were pretty big to be dolls. Meyer drove twelve miles south to the Deschutes County Sheriff's Office, in Terrbonne.

Since the gorge was the delineation between two counties—Deschutes County and Jefferson County—the sheriff's departments in both counties were notified, as well as the state police and police in the small towns of Redmond and Madras.

Later that day, volunteer firefighters scaled down the cliff of the canyon and found Larry and Marty. At least one man was injured when he slipped down part of the steep wall of the gorge. It took about five hours to take the broken and battered bodies back up to the top of the gorge. Photos of the children were taken both at the floor of the canyon and at the coroner's office.

One of the volunteer firefighters also had a job driving the station wagon for Ronald Toms Funeral Home so he took the children's bodies there. At 9:30 p.m. Dr. George McGeary began the autopsies. He concluded that both children showed evidence of "wounds suffered before they were thrown over the precipice." He wrote that whoever killed them had deliberately mutilated them first to make it appear they had been sexually assaulted by a man.

It took a few days to identify the children. No frantic parents had contacted the police to report their son and daughter missing. The police searched roads and fields near the gorge for evidence and contacted informants who were "known to associate with colored subjects" or "were of questionable moral character." State troopers showed photos of the dead children around, but they had no leads.

ON THEIR WAY BACK TO OAKLAND, Jeannace and Gertrude stopped in Cottage Grove to pick up Letha. Jeannace told her that Gertrude's children were in a foster home in Richmond, California. They arrived in Oakland on Saturday morning and found an efficiency apartment. Gertrude decided to sell the Mercury so they could rent a bigger place. That same afternoon they took the Mercury to a used car lot where Gertrude, who had hoped to get $80 for it, but left with $50. They rented an apartment with two bedrooms, one for Gertrude and one for Jeannace and Letha. Gertrude began to talk about her dream of moving to San Francisco.

Jeannace bought a newspaper and read about the unidentified bodies found in the gorge.

On the same morning the women arrived in Oakland, Red heard a news report on the radio. The bodies of two children had been found at the bottom of the Crooked River Gorge. Red knew that the mysterious early morning arrival of Jennace and Gertrude, the cleaning of the car, and the story about leaving Gertrude's children somewhere was suspicious.

"Red came out and told us, They found two bodies under the Crooked River Bridge,'" Ronn remembered. "I instantly knew that

Jen was involved. His fear was that Jen and Gertrude had taken up with a guy who had killed the children."

Despite his fear that his stepdaughter was mixed up in something horrific, Red put his two teenage sons in his car and drove to the home of a constable. Red told him he thought he knew who the two children were and gave them the women's names, the make of car they were driving, and where they were headed. State troopers went to Red's house and sifted through the ashes in the stove. They found remnants of clothing and the sole of a child's shoe. State police located a neighbor of Gertrude's in Eugene. They drove over the mountains to get her and took her back to central Oregon to try and identify their bodies. She did.

In Oakland, two detectives, Jim Spence and Leonard Fake, saw a teletype report about the children being found murdered. Spence had grown up near the gorge and kept the report, mostly out of curiosity. Then came more teletypes, including one stating that the women Oregon was looking for were possibly headed to Oakland. Finding them became a cause for him.

While searching for Gertrude and Jeannace, they found Dempsey Otis Jackson, who they described as "a drugged out, unemployed hod carrier." They showed him photos taken of the dead children. "They might be mine," was all he said.

Two days later the police found and arrested Jeannace, Gertrude and Letha. They found bloody clothing in the apartment and when they impounded the Mercury from the car lot, they found traces of blood in it.

While awaiting extradition, both women confessed, although they told wildly different stories.

After word of the arrests got back to Oregon, "Central Oregon mothers began to relax," *The Oregonian* reported. "The thought that a sex deviate might be on the loose had built up an almost tangible tension. Mothers were keeping their children close to home. No one wanted to trust them to babysitters."

JEFFERSON COUNTY SHERIFF S.E. SUMMERFIELD AND A police matron went to Oakland and drove the three women back north. There was little conversation.

Jeannace was incarcerated in the Deschutes County Jail in Bend, and Gertrude and Letha were the first residents of the new city jail on the ground floor of the Jefferson County Courthouse in Madras.

A grand jury indicted the two women on two charges each of first-degree murder. Jeannace pleaded not guilty, and Gertrude pleaded not guilty by reason of insanity. The county stalled bringing charges against Letha.

On June 9, Larry and Marty were buried in Mt. Jefferson Memorial Park Cemetery in Madras. A graveside service—kept secret from reporters—led by Rev. William Stone of St. Patrick's Catholic Church in Madras was attended by Gertrude, Letha, two jail matrons, the mortician and Sheriff Summerfield.

As the summer passed, court-appointed attorneys and the district attorney prepared for two trials. Then, during a routine hearing, Gertrude shocked the judge, her attorneys, the prosecutor, and the few spectators present when she suddenly confessed in open court to participating in the killing of four-year-old Martha. She admitted lifting the girl from the car, taking her blouse off, and throwing her into the canyon. But she claimed the girl had not been mutilated.

She said she was "under the domination of Miss Freeman and would do anything Miss Freeman wanted her to do."

Three psychiatrists and a clinical psychologist agreed. A judge would, too.

Both women were driven to Portland for psychiatric exams. In 1961, homosexuality was considered a sickness and all the doctors agreed. One of the psychiatrists who examined Jeannace considered lesbianism to be "an incontrovertible sign of a decaying personality."

Jeannace was labeled as a "sociopath-dissociate." Gertrude was officially diagnosed as an "easily manipulated simple schizophrenic" and "actively psychotic."

BECAUSE OF THE SEXUAL ASPECTS that were sure to be mentioned during Jeannace's trial, as well as the gruesome killings of the children, no one under the age of twelve was permitted in the courtroom. One of the defense attorneys wondered if the eight men and four women on the jury even *knew* what homosexuality was.

Covering the case was a challenge for newspapers. Editors had to watch for graphic details reporters tried to include, including the fact that one of the women had licked the tire iron after using it on Larry and Marty. The papers didn't know how to refer to the women. Some chose the euphemisms "girlfriend" or "companion" to describe their relationship. It would be twenty years before an article updating the case used the term "lesbian lovers."

In addition to the farmers and townspeople who crowded the courtroom, several "tough-looking in females in leather, sporting tattoos and short haircuts" began to appear, hoping to send words of support to Jeannace.

Jeannace's attorneys cleaned her up before her trial. Gone was the slicked back hair, the cowboy boots, the tight jeans and swagger. She appeared in court wearing a dark skirt, white blouse, and a checked sweater. The unfamiliar clothes made her fidget. One thing her attorneys couldn't prevent—she smoked cigars during breaks.

ON THURSDAY, SEPTEMBER 7, 1961 DISTRICT ATTORNEY Warren H. Albright gave his opening statement to the jury considering Jeannace's fate. He said that Larry and Marty had been killed because they had interfered with the "homosexual arrangement" between the two women. He said that Jeannace had killed Larry, and Gertrude had killed Marty.

The judge told the jury it would be sequestered for the duration of the trial. And then they boarded a bus and were driven to the canyon and stood at the same guardrail where the children had been thrown over.

A state patrol car drove Jeannace to the scene, too. She showed no emotion as she looked out over the canyon and as she watched the jurors talk quietly among themselves.

Gertrude testified against Jeannace at her trial.

After a ten-day trial and seven hours of deliberation, the jury found Jeannace guilty of first-degree murder. Because the jury did not ask for a recommendation for leniency, the sentence was mandatory: death. The Oregon State Penitentiary in Salem began preparing a cell for her. It had never had a woman on death row. When she left Madras to be transferred to Salem, Jeannace shook hands with Sheriff Summerfield.

While Gertrude awaited sentencing, she gave an interview to *The Bend Bulletin.* Chain-smoking Camels, drinking coffee, and smiling for the camera, Gertrude remembered her childhood "as a happy one, with good parents and no hardships." Letha, described as a bird-like, black-haired girl weighing less than 100 pounds, was in a cell near Gertrude's and was also interviewed. Neither could talk about the crime but the reporter remarked on Letha's pencil sketches and paintings covering the walls of her cell, including an "amazing" likeness of Jacqueline Kennedy. The police finally released her since she wasn't in the car when the children were murdered.

Gertrude had gained weight in jail and the police matron told the reporter that Gertrude liked to nibble candy while she read "adventure tales" set in Canada, Africa and Alaska. Gertrude's own dream, she told the reporter, was simpler. She wanted to one day own a chicken ranch in California.

The reporter concluded the interview by asking if Gertrude had any advice for young girls. She did.

"Be careful who you make friends with. Think what you are getting into before you take any decided steps. Know people that you take into your confidence. Keep the commandments of the good Lord above all things.'"

Because Gertrude pleaded guilty, she had no trial. A month after Jeannace's trial, Circuit Judge Robert H. Foley sentenced

Gertrude to life in prison. Now referred to as Mrs. Nunez by the newspapers—because she'd never been divorced from her husband, and hadn't married the man who fathered her children—Gertrude wore the same flowered dress she'd worn during earlier court appearances. The defense attorneys, all appointed to represent Jeannace and Gertrude, saw their hair turn gray during the fall. They worried about what defending the women would do to their careers.

The decision to spare Gertrude's life shocked the community, which wanted to see both women executed. But it was the State of Oregon that asked Judge Foley to sentence Gertrude to life in prison for the murder of her daughter. Three psychiatrists and a clinical psychologist agreed: Jeannace had planned and directed the crime. The same psychiatrist who called Jeannace "a very severe sociopath," testified that Gertrude was "passive, submissive, dependent, ignorant, gullible and suggestible." Therefore, she deserved a different sentence.

Like a lot of the citizens of Central Oregon, Jeannace's brother Ronn Witcraft felt Gertrude's sentence was unfair. If his sister Jenny got the death penalty, so should Gertrude.

"Was Jeannace guilty? Absolutely, she told me so," he said decades later. "But what mother could let someone do that to their child? Jenny was a victim of a society. Society did not have ability to understand that some girls are different."

Attorneys helped Jeannace with appeals. Her legal counsel argued that Jeannace was "a poorly educated, indigent, nineteen-year-old girl," at the time of the crime, and had been "held in custody for eighteen days before counsel was appointed for her," which wasn't until she was arraigned. The Oregon Supreme Court ruled that there was no unlawful delay in bringing her before a magistrate, and that there was no constitutional obligation to furnish counsel prior to arraignment.

Jeannace Freeman was not executed. But she came close. The state set several execution dates but new attorneys working on her behalf got stays of execution. In another state, at another time, with another governor, she might have died. Mark Hatfield, a staunch opponent of capital punishment, had been elected governor in 1958. In 1964, 60 percent of Oregon voters weighed in against capital punishment, and Jeannace's sentence was commuted to life in prison. She served twenty-four years, some of it in California. She was initially freed in 1983, but went back to prison for violating her parole by living with a woman in Bellingham, Washington who had children.

When she was released again in 1985 she gave an interview to a Bend newspaper that was also printed in the *Register-Guard* of Eugene. She said she "used to have a real bad attitude" but had grown up. She had learned a trade, welding. And she confessed something—that she came close to killing Gertrude at the Crooked River Bridge. They were arguing about murdering the children and about Jeannace's relationship with Letha, and for an instant Jeannace had planned to hit Gertrude with the lug wrench they used on the children.

GERTRUDE JACKSON was paroled after serving seven years in prison. Not much is known about the rest of her life, except that she suffered from "moments of recklessness, psychotic delusions, paranoid violence, attachments to destructive people, and chronic dissociation," according to documents.

Longtime Portland reporter Paul Hanson met with Gertrude in the early 1980s when he was considering writing a book. She had changed her name. She was nearly sixty years old, gray, and her demeanor was "flat" and "blas ." As Gertrude talked about the crime and her relationship with Jeannace, Hanson thought it seemed as if she was still in love with the woman she hadn't seen in nearly twenty-five years. Either before or after Hanson met with her, Gertrude had a psychotic break and tried to stab a man with a ballpoint pen at a dry cleaning business.

A few years later, unbeknownst to the community that had wanted to throw *her* off the Crooked River Bridge, Gertrude was living in Madras and working as a babysitter. One day, as she was being driven across the bridge, she had another psychotic break. After trying to start a fire in a room at Mountain View Hospital in Madras, she was committed for a year to the state mental hospital in Salem.

Three years later, in 1986, she died.

Hanson also met Jeannace when she was still incarcerated at the penitentiary in Salem. What began as a pleasant conversation in the cafeteria took a bad turn.

"We asked her which version of what happened that night she wanted us to print, and that ended things pretty quickly," Hanson remembers. "I will say she was the single most frightening human being I have ever encountered."

IN THE EARLY 1990s, ABOUT THIRTY YEARS AFTER THE CROOKED RIVER BRIDGE MURDERS, Jeannace wanted to go to Madras to see the graves of two of her siblings who died young, as well as visit Red's grave.

Ronn drove her north on Highway 97. They probably sang "their song," "Our Day Will Come" during the trip. As they approached the gorge, Jenny asked him to stop.

Ronn and Jeannace walked along the edge of the canyon. "She cried hard, deep sobs," Ronn remembered. "I held her. She didn't really indicate she was going to throw herself off but I think she was thinking about it. She was very remorseful."

Jeannace, who changed her name to Wilma Lin Rhule—Rhule was her mother's surname—was arrested for the last time in 2002 for threatening two acquaintances with a knife and forcing them to drive her to a store. She had been working as a driver for an escort business that provided services to an area outside of Eugene near her beloved McKenzie River.

Jeannace Freeman died in 2003 of emphysema and lung cancer while an inmate of Coffee Creek Correctional Facility in Wilsonville, Oregon. She was sixty-two and was still known as "the most despised woman" in Oregon and the instigator of "the crime of the century." She was cremated and her family celebrated her life by sending her ashes on a small float adorned with roses down her beloved McKenzie River, the place she loved to fish and was most at peace.

The people of Madras and Redmond still talk about the murders. They drop their voices and whisper when they talk about Jeannace and Gertrude being lesbians, and continue to insist there were no homosexuals in the community until the fateful morning the two women stopped their car at the Crooked River Bridge.

For the first time since Jeannace Freeman, there is another woman on death row in Oregon. Angela McAnulty—who is the subject of another chapter in this collection of notorious crimes — was sentenced to death for starving and torturing her fifteen-year-old daughter to death.

For now, McAnulty is safe. The state's governor has placed a moratorium on executions.

A new Crooked River Bridge was completed in 2000, and the old one is open to pedestrians. They both give a breathtaking view to motorists crossing the gorge. Sometimes people stop to picnic. The bridge's scenic viewpoint is named for Peter Skeen Ogden, a fur trader, explorer and Indian fighter in the 1820s. On a plaque with the history of the area there is no mention of the bridge's most infamous crime. But near the wall where Jeannace and Gertrude threw the children over there's a sign that shows a dog leaping off the cliff into thin air and a few cautionary words:

Warning—Hazardous cliffs. Many dogs have died here!

Christian Longo
The Narcissist

A HANDSOME MAN, GOOD AT LYING, CHEATING AND STEALING but a bad husband and father, murders his pretty wife and three young children. He escapes to a beach in Mexico, makes the FBI's Ten Most Wanted List, assumes the identity of a disgraced journalist, is captured, and is sentenced to death.

It's always seemed like a movie. Now it is.

To Oregonians, Christian Longo is and will always be a narcissistic monster—even if he's portrayed by actor James Franco in a film produced by Brad Pitt's production company. In the summer of 2013, the movie of Longo's crimes, time on the run, and capture, titled *True Story*, was being shot thirty-seven miles north of Manhattan. It really happened in Newport, a quiet year-round fishing community on the central Oregon coast.

Most years there are no murders or tragic accidents in Newport. But the winter of 2001 was brutal. The day before Thanksgiving, two teenagers, a boyfriend and girlfriend, were swept out to sea while walking on the beach. In December, four local crabbers died when their fishing boat overturned.

On December 19, the community was still reeling from those deaths when a man at an RV park spotted the body of a young boy floating face down in an inlet twelve miles south of Newport. The child had slipped free of a *Rugrats* pillow case with a rock that had been tied to his ankle to weigh him down. Three days later, the body of a small girl was discovered with a rock in a floral pillowcase tied to her ankle. Both children were in underpants.

The next week divers found two suitcases under a dock at a Newport condominium complex. One had the body of a naked woman, the other the body of a young girl. Eventually, police identified them as mother and children, the Longo family. They were five-year-old Zachary, three-year-old Sadie Ann, two-year-old Madison, and thirty-four-year-old MaryJane Longo. The family had lived briefly in the condo.

A local minister described Newport as "raw with loss."

Initially, the police just wanted to question Christian Longo, husband and father to the dead family, wherever he was.

Within a day, they had charged him with murdering his family.

TALL, WITH REDDISH-BLOND HAIR, Christian Longo was boyishly good-looking, despite a wide jaw and large ears. He was raised by strict Jehovah's Witness parents in Michigan. As a teenager he took part in door-to-door ministry. At nineteen, he met MaryJane Baker in the church parking lot. She was seven years older and had qualms about his immaturity, but they married five months later. She was petite and pretty with curly dark hair.

There were always money problems. When he couldn't keep up with the payments on a three-and-a-half-carat diamond engagement ring, he stole money from a camera store where he worked. He said his conscience got the better of him and he left a check for the amount and a resignation letter at the store the next day. The church learned about the incident and he wasn't allowed to marry MaryJane in the Kingdom Hall.

It was important to Longo's ego to be thought of as successful, to keep up appearances. But by the time the couple's three children arrived in quick succession, Christian had maxed out their credit on new cars, nice clothes, and various businesses. He got his father to invest tens of thousands of dollars in a construction cleanup business that started strong but soon failed.

Whatever money he got his hands on went for a boat, two jet skis—he told friends he'd won them in a contest—and two new cars. He became good at deception, at least short-term deception. After one of the cars was towed away and the other broke down, he created a fake driver's license, took a new Pontiac minivan for a test drive, and never returned the car to the dealership. When

MaryJane asked why they weren't receiving bills for the new car, he created bogus ones on a computer and mailed them to their home.

In 2000, MaryJane told her sister that she thought Christian was having an affair. He admitted it, and told her he no longer loved her and hadn't since she began having children. But MaryJane stayed with her husband.

In September 2000, Longo was arrested for faking checks from companies that owed his business money. He pleaded guilty and received three years' probation. He was forced out of the Jehovah's Witnesses because of the forgeries.

Longo promised MaryJane he'd be truthful and they'd start over. But first, there was a last hurrah; he took scuba diving lessons and paid for her to have corrective eye surgery. Then, convincing her that a new start meant moving, they went to Ohio where they lived in a warehouse that he kept promising to renovate. He wrote more bad checks in Ohio, then packed up the family again, leaving in a hurry just before he was to be arrested for violating probation for the forgery conviction. He was also being sued for not paying thousands of dollars of loans, car-lease payments and restitution for selling a stolen trailer.

On the way west, they sold MaryJane's engagement ring, the one he'd stolen money to buy. MaryJane didn't know she was driving a stolen SUV and Longo was driving a rental truck that wasn't supposed to leave Ohio. By then her parents and sisters had lost touch with her and filed a missing-persons report. The family bounced around different towns on the Oregon coast, being evicted when they couldn't pay their rent. They were as far west as they could go.

Wherever they lived, MaryJane stayed at home with the children. As the oldest, five-year-old Zachery had dark hair and looked like his mother. The girls were both blonde; three-year-old Sadie Ann sometimes wore her hair in pigtails. In photographs, Sadie Ann and Zachery were often posed on either side of two-year-old Madison, as if to protect her if they could.

In December 2001, Christian was working part-time at a

Starbucks caf at a Fred Meyer. He wasn't earning nearly enough to support a family of five, even after he was promoted to working at Fred Meyer. The night of December 16, he stood on the balcony of the condo in Newport and looked at the bay. They were to be evicted yet again the next day.

It was, he said later, "the beginning of the end."

THAT NIGHT, Christian Longo strangled his family. He stuffed Madison and Mary Jane into two suitcases, and dumped them into the ocean. Then he drove fifteen minutes south and threw the bodies of Zachery and Sadie off a bridge into the Lint Slough. He left large bags of toys, books, family photos, children's clothes and MaryJane's wallet in a Dumpster. On the seventeenth, Longo stole a car, went to his gym, and showed up at his job. He went to a Starbucks Christmas party at a pizza place.

He told co-workers that his wife had left him for another man. Two days later, after hearing a news report that the body of a boy had been discovered, Longo picked up his last paycheck and drove to San Francisco.

In San Francisco he applied for another job at Starbucks but instead of taking the job, he used a credit card number he'd stolen in Newport to buy a plane ticket to Cancun, Mexico. He rented a cabana, found a girlfriend—a German woman who wanted to be a photographer— smoked pot, and pretended to be a journalist. He picked a real-life writer, Michael Finkel, who that same week was fired as a contributor to *The New York Times* after it had been learned that he faked much of a magazine cover story about a young African plantation worker.

Longo had followed Finkel's work in *Skiing, National Geographic Adventure, Sports Illustrated, and The New York Times*, as the journalist had reported from as far afield as Gaza and Haiti.

Police found Longo's car at the San Francisco airport. The FBI put Christian Longo on its Ten Most Wanted list—Osama bin Laden was on it, too—and MaryJane's family participated in an episode of *America's Most Wanted*. He stayed for a while at a youth hostel in

Cancun but was told to leave after some money was stolen. He went from there to Tulum, a coastal town of "modest resorts."

A Canadian woman called the FBI after recognizing Longo. He was arrested Sunday, January 13, 2002.

He was returned to the Lincoln County Jail in Newport. "He always seemed pleasant," said a woman who managed the condo complex where the Longos had rented. "He was well dressed, well groomed, and well mannered. He was a nice guy."

Not everybody along the coast had good memories of him. One landlord said Longo had stolen two crab traps.

CHRISTIAN LONGO PLEADED GUILTY TO MURDERING MaryJane and Madison, but refused to enter a plea on charges of killing Sadie and Zachery. The jury would decide if he was also guilty of murdering the other two children and if he should die by lethal injection.

He was his own key witness. Taking the stand, Longo described how on the night of December 16, he came home from work, had some wine and cheese, and stayed up late telling MaryJane the truth about the stolen van and lack of rent money. He said she was angry and emotional, that she slapped him and berated him.

At first he blamed an intruder on drugs for killing his family. Then he claimed that MaryJane had killed the two older children, which prompted him to kill her and their youngest child. In the process of putting their bodies in the suitcases, he found that two-year-old Madison was still breathing. He strangled her until she wasn't, and added some of her clothes to the suitcase "to make it more comfortable" for the dead girl.

Prosecutors never believed that MaryJane had played a part in the killings. They pointed out that she weighed only 110 pounds, had no history of violence and would have been unable to throw her children into the water with heavy rocks attached. They proved that Longo had been preparing to kill his family for a long time. He'd been researching different methods of murder online. He was preparing aliases. Prosecutors said he had left behind a lot of the family's personal belongings in Ohio.

Prosecutors summed up Longo this way: He was "an ice-cold, calculating serial liar who grew tired of his family."

ON APRIL 7, 2003, A JURY FOUND CHRISTIAN LONGO GUILTY OF murdering Zachery and Sadie. A week later, the same jury sentenced Longo to death for all four killings.

Longo may never be executed. There have been no executions carried out in Oregon in fourteen years, in part because the state's current governor has imposed a moratorium on them.

Longo has kept himself in the limelight. Some of his letters—mostly to women who write to him—have been obtained by the news media. In one letter in 2012, Longo wrote about his trial and seemed to confess:

"I got up on the stand and essentially blamed my wife for everything. I was still stuck in a phase where I couldn't fathom the thought of me being capable of doing what I was convicted of."

He also wrote that he "almost" totally agreed with a psychologist who had concluded he had a narcissistic personality disorder.

In a "truth is stranger than fiction" development, he cooperated with Michael Finkel—to whom he had played doppelganger—on a book and an article in *Esquire*.

After serving just five years in prison, Longo decided to abandon his legal appeals. Being put to death, he stated, was preferable to spending life in a six-foot-by-eight-foot cell. Then he did an abrupt about-face.

According to Michael Finkel, Longo is a sensitive man who got "choked up" when he saw the movies *E.T.* and *Titanic*. But it was the Will Smith film *Seven Pounds*—which he saw on a seven-inch TV screen in his cell—that gave Longo a raison d'être.

In the movie, Smith's character has caused an automobile accident while texting, killing his fiancée and six strangers. He sets out to help seven people by donating his organs after he commits suicide. Longo was so moved by the movie that he and his brother set up an enterprise in 2011 called GAVE—Gifts of Anatomical Value from the Executed. (An Internet search finds that Longo and his brother have tinkered with the name and GAVE now stands for "Gifts of Anatomical Value from Everyone." Maybe the word executed' wasn't good marketing.)

Longo, who always aspired to be a writer, is now a published author. On March 5, 2011, *The New York Times* published an opinion piece by Longo in which he launched a national campaign to encourage states to let inmates on death row donate their organs after they've been executed.

Longo argued that 110,000 Americans are on organ waiting lists. Nineteen of them die each day. With more than 3,000 prisoners on death row in the U.S., one inmate could save up to eight lives by donating healthy lungs, kidneys, a liver, a heart and other transplantable organs.

There is no law barring inmates condemned to death from donating their organs, but no prisons permit it. Many states use a cocktail of three drugs in their lethal injections, which damage the organs. But Longo says there's a way around that. Oregon and Washington, for example, use a larger dose of one drug which doesn't affect the organs.

Longo has also written an e-book, *The Forsaken Gift of Life: An Expose of the Pointless Ban on Prisoner Organ Donation.*

He said his motive is to "save lives... not to set right my wrongs—as this is unfortunately impossible—but to make a positive out of an otherwise horrible situation." A headline in the *Eugene Register-Guard*, however, questioned if Longo's "crusade" was "just another selfish plea for attention."

MaryJane's family live for the day Longo is executed. But not for the reason he hopes, so he can donate his organs. They just want him dead.

As for the tall, still-boyish Longo, he's nearly forty years old and his hair is receding. He reportedly admitted to a federal agent years ago that his good looks had helped him get away with a lot of crimes.

"That's been my downfall," he said.

Thankfully, his good looks didn't let him get away with murder. It sounds like the plot of a movie.

My Day With Diane Downs
By Gregg Olsen

MUCH TO MY FAMILY'S CHAGRIN, I'VE CORRESPONDED WITH several well-known killers over the years, including Arthur Shawcross ("The Genesee River Killer"); Pamela Smart (the New Hampshire teacher convicted with her fifteen-year-old lover of the murder of her husband); Debora Green (who killed her two children in a house fire and fed her husband ricin); and Diane Downs, Oregon's most notorious female killer.

Some of you will remember the story—among many of its legacies, it coined the term Shaggy Haired Stranger or SHS.

Downs claimed that a SHS tried to hijack her car on a dirt road in Springfield on May 19, 1983. He shot her three children, eight-year-old Christie, seven-year-old Cheryl Ann, and three-year-old Danny, and also shot her in the arm. Cheryl died that evening at the hospital, Danny was left paralyzed, and Christie partly paralyzed. Downs was arrested, convicted, and sentenced to life plus fifty-five years.

She didn't fade away. Not this one. Diane Downs escaped prison for a memorable week during the early part of her incarceration. She famously appeared toe to toe with Oprah. And one of the most beautiful women in the world played her in a two-part miniseries (anyone remember the scene in which the Diane character rocked out to Duran Duran's "Hungry Like the Wolf" when it was played in court?).

Like other prisoners I've communicated with, Downs was focused—really manic, paranoid, obsessed—with her appeals and efforts to prove her innocence. In earlier years she had juggled media requests and now I was one of her "would-be suitors." She invited me to visit and promised that she was "much funnier in person."

How could I resist?

As many of you probably know, Downs has spent time in prisons in Oregon and New Jersey before being incarcerated in the Valley State Prison for Women in Chowchilla, California.

That's where I met with her on September 27, 2003, nineteen years after her conviction. I'll never forget her freakish charm, her vivid blue eyes, and her need to win people over. What did we talk about? Her, of course. After all, experts have diagnosed her as a "narcissistic psychopath."

With Downs it was all about her, twenty-four-seven.

Some of her letters to me were written in ink on yellow legal paper. Some are scribbled in pencil on the back of articles about me that her father had printed and sent to her.

In letters written before and after our meeting, she cautioned me that after hearing her out and reading materials she had collected, I would learn that "the true criminals are the cops."

Although she has told parole boards different versions of what happened on May 19, 1983, the version she explained to me in a letter is part of her recurring story:

The night of May 19, 1983, I received a phone call from someone who said I could pick up photos of illegal activity that would greatly please my boyfriend (he had told Downs he was a federal agent). As I approached the rendezvous spot a man flagged me down. He demanded my car. I laughed at him because his demand was so incongruous with my aim. He lunged at the car, shot my children. We struggled, he fell back and I fled in the car. I could not tell the police the reason I was out there was to pick up photos of their DA (Lane County D.A. Pat Horton) making drug deals. Not even the Feds knew who the bad cops were.

In some two dozen letters, she wrote to me about of how wronged she had been by the men who investigated and prosecuted her, including D.A. Pat Horton and Detective Doug Welch.

She claims that Horton had a conflict of interest, an "allegiance" to The Free Souls, a motorcycle club. She sent me copies of affidavits that implicate a drug dealer and a member of "The Free Souls" in the shootings of her children. According to his close friends, James Claire Haynes fit the description of a police sketch of a suspect, owned a yellow car like the one Downs described, and was believed to have sold Downs speed. She owed him money, they said, a motive for stopping her car on a country road to scare her.

Her appeals had been hampered by the fact that police reports on many aspects of the investigation, including phone logs and information on suspects like Haynes, went missing.

Doug Welch lied to judges and the Attorney General and to my attorneys and investigator and the media about those reports. He swung from "they never existed" to "they were destroyed." Even as he stood over the 4,700 documents, he creatively denied their existence. Literally 4,700 documents at his feet and Doug said he meant that Lane County Sheriff's Office did not have any physical evidence.

William J. Teesdale, an investigator for the Federal Public Defender's Office in Oregon, spent 1997 and 1998 trying to get access to materials in the Lane County Sheriff's Department's evidence room, including finger print information, the evidence log, and court transcripts. What he got was the runaround. In a 1998 affidavit, Teesdale stated that he was told by Det. Welch that "all of the physical evidence in the Downs case had been destroyed," and that there were no notes of police reports or suspect leads still in existence. Welch claimed they were destroyed in 1997—about the time Teesdale began trying to get access to them.

However, Teesdale found them, boxes and boxes and boxes of physical evidence, exhibits, police reports, information on suspects, documents and photographs, nearly 5,000 pages worth.

At one time, she and her legal team pursued other theories that would prove Downs innocent. The weapon was never found, and the markings on the bullet casings didn't match the markings on cartridges in her apartment. Danny drew a sketch of a man holding a gun in his left hand—she is right-handed. She sent me a copy of Danny's drawing.

None of the findings have changed her status but are proof, as she told me, that "the true criminals are the cops." That's the biggest source of Downs's grudge. But she holds others, too.

Welch told ___ that I basically tried to seduce him on the way to prison! Get real !! I was chained up in a cage. The only thing on my mind was what I'd be faced with in prison. But HE wants to believe I'd "care" enough to seduce him?!

Here's a secret for you, Gregg. I don't seduce men. I let them seduce me, then I choose the one I want and there's NO WAY I'd want a man who lied about me in court for the purpose of illegally imprisoning me... you can presume the truth is Welch wished I'd seduced him—but I sure didn't. The man strove to destroy me. And he does so to this day.

In articles and books—and in the 1989 made-for-TV movie about her, *Small Sacrifices*—Downs is depicted as highly sexual. (She told me that Farrah Fawcett, who portrayed her in the movie, wasn't pretty enough for the role.) She always juggled lovers. She admitted that her husband Steve was not Danny's father (they were divorced in 1980, a year after Danny was born). And she was pregnant by an unknown man while she stood trial. Her reason for attempting to kill her children, prosecutors claimed, was because her married lover didn't want children.

Even in her letters, she is candid about her sexuality.

How do I say this delicately? Sexually, I'm not your run-of-the-mill female. There's a reason "Lew" (not his real name) would leave his wife's bed at 5 a.m. to come to my apartment to wake me up.

The letters tapered off and ended in 2006. Downs always insisted that the story that should be told is that of her parents. They continue to work to prove her innocence. On his web page DianeDowns.com, her father, Wes Frederickson, is offering a $100,000 reward for the capture of the "real killer."

SEE YOU IN 2020.

That's what Oregon said to Diane Downs at her last parole hearing in 2010. She'll be sixty-five years old in 2020. She looks older than her age. Her once-blonde shag is white, and as *The Oregonian* wrote after her 2010 parole hearing, she is "nearly unrecognizable from the bombshell blonde who once flounced unashamed past television news cameras in handcuffs and shackles."

She continues to frustrate the Oregon parole board, maintaining her innocence and telling at least three versions of what happened that night, blaming a "bushy-haired stranger," two men wearing ski masks, and corrupt law enforcement officials for the shootings. Labeled a "dangerous offender" with a "severe personality disorder," she has spent much of her time plotting how to get out of prison, including one plan to commandeer a helicopter. She escaped from the Oregon Women's Correctional Center in Salem for ten days in 1987 and was later transferred out of state. Twice she tried to escape from a New Jersey prison and once from the California prison in 1994.

She told the parole board that the escape attempts are evidence of her "healthy attitude about society" and that she is ready for parole.

They didn't agree.

As for Diane's children, prosecutor Fred Hugi (who Downs does not fault for her conviction) and his wife adopted Danny and Christie. The baby Downs gave birth to in prison was put up for adoption. Now a single mother in Bend, Rebecca Babcock told *Oprah* and *20/20* that she found out about her parentage from a babysitter when she was a child.

Several years ago, Babcock wrote her mother. The result was a string of "bizarre," "paranoid" letters from Downs. When Babcock asked her biological mother to never write to her again, the response was a scathing letter telling her that her son would grow up to be a killer.

As far as I know, mother and daughter don't write any more.

And me? I'm off the Christmas card list too.

OREGON PHOTO ARCHIVE

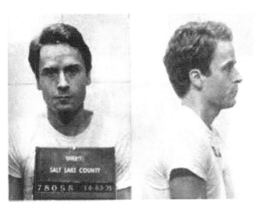

Ted Bundy in Utah in October, 1975, charged with the attempted kidnapping and attempted homicide of Carol DaRonch. She was lucky—she escaped from his car. Not many did. By this time he had killed at least 12 young women in Oregon, Washington, Colorado, Utah and possibly Idaho.

Jerome Henry Brudos, who started his criminal career by choking women and stealing their shoes. He moved on to murder.

Randall Woodfield, the "I-5 Bandit," named for a string of murders he committed along the freeway corridor.

Jeannette Maples was a quiet, shy 15-year old when she died an especially cruel death—tortured and starved by her mother.

Angela McAnulty tortured her daughter so severely the girl's bones were exposed. Her husband Richard, Jeannette's step-father, looked the other way. Angela McAnulty is the first woman to reside on Oregon's death row in 50 years.

A poster publicizing the disappearance of 7-year-old Kyron Horman from his Portland school on June 4, 2010. In the last photo taken of him, he proudly shows off his science exhibit.

In the early days after Kyron's disappearance his parents and step-parents spoke as one to the media. Suspicion quickly fell on Kyron's step-mother, Terri Horman. Left to right: Kyron's mother Desiree Young, step-mother Terri Horman, father Kaine Horman, step-father Tony Young.

The Crooked River Bridge and canyon near Madras, site of Oregon's most sensational murder. The canyon is 27 stories deep. Two children thrown over the edge didn't stand a chance.

Nineteen year old Jeannace Freeman usually wore tight jeans, slicked her hair back, and bound her breasts so she could pass as a man. Her attorneys made her look more feminine for her trial.

The members of the Longo family who were found murdered on the Oregon coast.

MaryJane Longo and her children, Zachary, Sadie Ann and Madison, all murdered by Christian Longo when he saw no way out from his years of personal and professional failures.

Christian Longo was finally captured in Mexico, where he had assumed the identity of a former New York Times journalist.

Diane Downs with her children Danny, Christie and Cheryl Ann shortly before she claimed a "bushy-haired stranger" flagged down her car on a country road near Springfield and shot them on May 19, 1983.

Downs was found guilty and sentenced to 55 years in prison. She escaped from the state prison in Salem for several days in 1987.

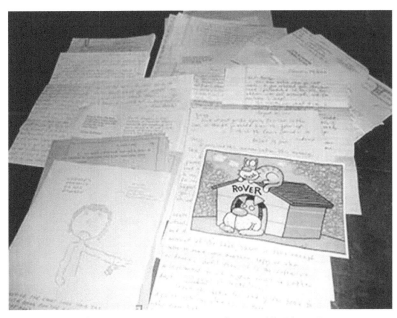

Some of Gregg Olsen's correspondence with Diane Downs. He spent a day with her at the Valley State Prison for Women in Chowchilla, California in 2003.

Oregon's parole board is frustrated that Downs maintains her innocence in the shooting of her children. She told them that her escape attempts are evidence of her "healthy attitude about society" and that she is ready for parole. They don't agree.

Don't Miss These Kindle Unlimited Reads by New York Times Bestselling Author Gregg Olsen!

The true story of Sharon Nelson, the woman who had her lover murder two of her three husbands, and a box set of cases from the Notorious USA, New York Times Bestselling Series

Made in United States
Cleveland, OH
04 January 2025

13068233R00042